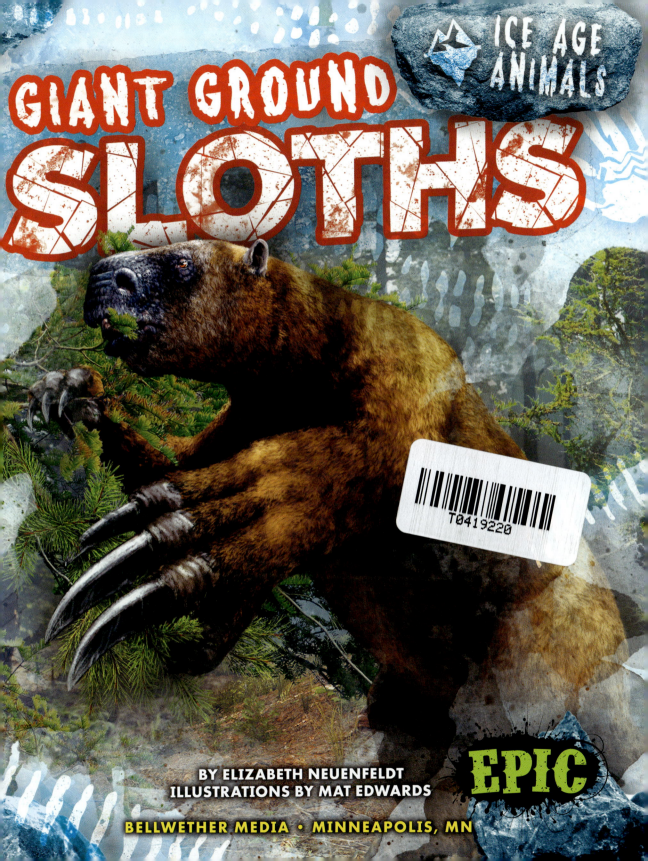

GIANT GROUND SLOTHS

ICE AGE ANIMALS

EPIC

BY ELIZABETH NEUENFELDT
ILLUSTRATIONS BY MAT EDWARDS

BELLWETHER MEDIA • MINNEAPOLIS, MN

EPIC

EPIC BOOKS are no ordinary books. They burst with intense action, high-speed heroics, and shadows of the unknown. Are you ready for an Epic adventure?

This edition first published in 2025 by Bellwether Media, Inc.

No part of this publication may be reproduced in whole or in part without written permission of the publisher. For information regarding permission, write to Bellwether Media, Inc., Attention: Permissions Department, 6012 Blue Circle Drive, Minnetonka, MN 55343.

Library of Congress Cataloging-in-Publication Data

Names: Neuenfeldt, Elizabeth, author. Title: Giant ground sloths / by Elizabeth Neuenfeldt.
Description: Minneapolis, MN : Bellwether Media, Inc., 2025. | Series: Epic: Ice age animals |
Includes bibliographical references and index. | Audience: Ages 7-12 | Audience: Grades 2-3 |
Summary: "Engaging images accompany information about giant ground sloths. The combination of
  high-interest subject matter and light text is intended for students in grades 2 through 7"--
  Provided by publisher.
Identifiers: LCCN 2024019779 (print) | LCCN 2024019780 (ebook) | ISBN 9798893040418 |
  ISBN 9798893041606 (paperback) | ISBN 9781644879818 (ebook)
Subjects: LCSH: Megatherium--Juvenile literature. | Sloths, Fossil--Juvenile literature. |
  Ground sloths--Juvenile literature.
Classification: LCC QE882.E2 N48 2025 (print) | LCC QE882.E2 (ebook) |
  DDC 569/.31--dc23/eng/20240509
LC record available at https://lccn.loc.gov/2024019779
LC ebook record available at https://lccn.loc.gov/2024019780

Editor: Betsy Rathburn   Designer: Jeffrey Kollock

Printed in the United States of America, North Mankato, MN.

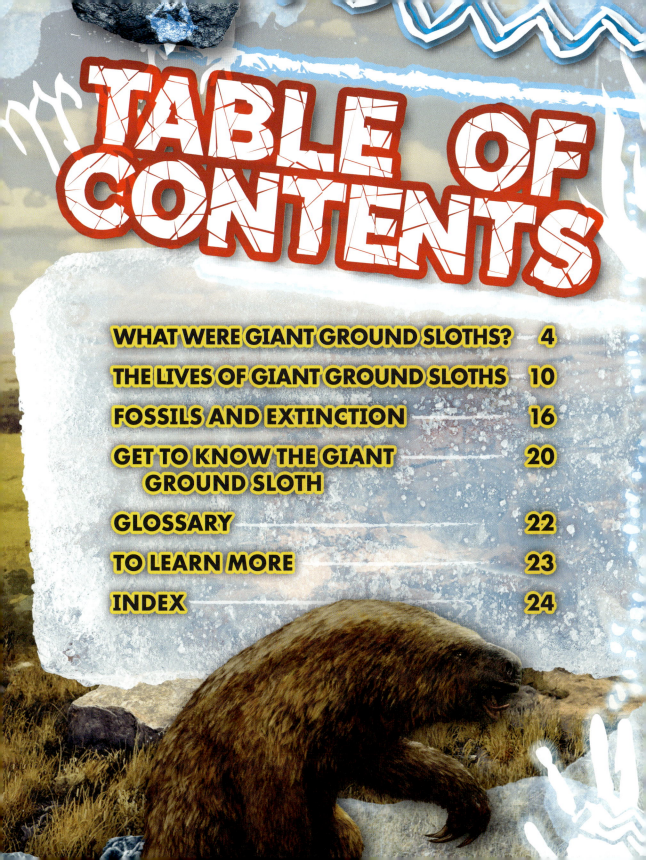

TABLE OF CONTENTS

WHAT WERE GIANT GROUND SLOTHS?

Giant ground sloths were big **mammals**. They first lived during the **Eocene epoch**. That was around 35 million years ago!

4

GIANT GROUND SLOTH RANGE MAP

EARTH

● = range

WHEN
First lived during the Eocene epoch

There were many **species** of giant ground sloths. They lived across North and South America.

Giant ground sloths had long fur. Some had tiny bones under their fur. These protected them from **predators**! Giant ground sloths had long claws and strong back legs. Their short tails helped them **balance**.

predators

long claws

Giant ground sloth species were different sizes. The largest weighed more than 8,000 pounds (3,629 kilograms).

8

Some reached 11.5 feet (3.5 meters) tall on their back legs!

GIANT GROUND SLOTH SIZE COMPARISON

11.5 feet (3.5 meters) tall on back legs

10 feet (3 meters)

5 feet (1.5 meters)

REFRIGERATORS

GIANT GROUND SLOTH

HUMANS

THE LIVES OF GIANT GROUND SLOTHS

Many giant ground sloths were **herbivores**. They ate fruit, grass, and leaves. They stood on their back legs to reach food in trees. They used their claws to dig for food. Some species were **omnivores**. They also ate meat.

GIANT GROUND SLOTH DIET

TYPE

herbivores

omnivores

fruit

grass

leaves

meat

PLANTING WITH POOP

Some sloths ate fruit from Joshua trees. They later pooped out Joshua tree seeds. This helped more Joshua trees grow!

Some giant ground sloths lived alone. Others may have lived in groups.

young giant ground sloth

Giant ground sloths dug **burrows**. They also lived in caves. Females gave birth to live young. Young sloths stayed close to their mom.

burrow

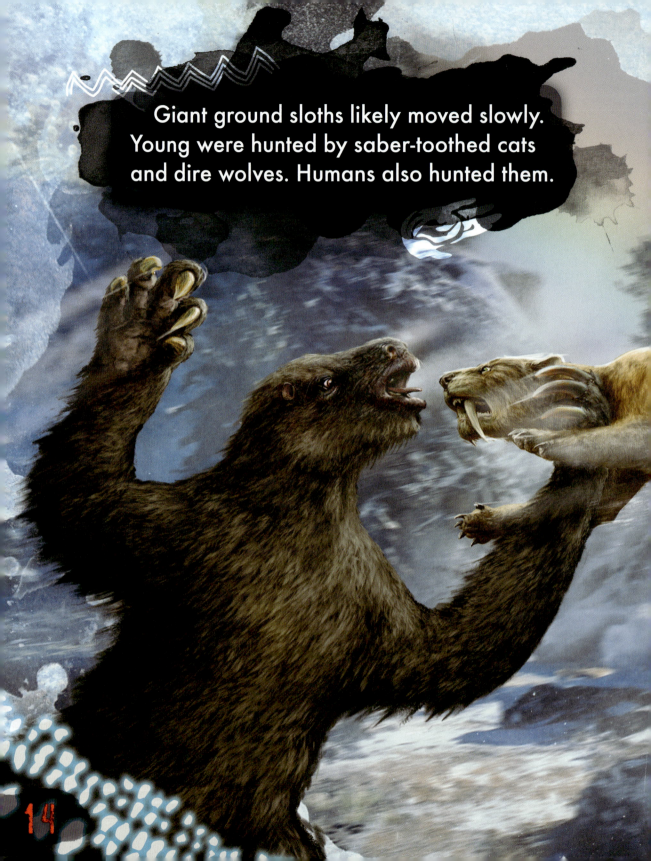

Giant ground sloths likely moved slowly. Young were hunted by saber-toothed cats and dire wolves. Humans also hunted them.

Giant ground sloths fought enemies with their claws.

saber-toothed cat

FOSSILS AND EXTINCTION

A PRESIDENTIAL SLOTH

Jefferson's ground sloth is named after the third United States president, Thomas Jefferson. He studied the sloth's fossils!

FAMOUS FOSSIL FIND

WHEN
1780s

FOUND BY
Manuel Torres

FAMOUS FOR
First known giant ground sloth fossil

WHERE
Argentina

SOUTH AMERICA

Giant ground sloths began to go **extinct** around 10,000 years ago. This was likely caused by humans and Earth's changing **climate**. Giant ground sloth **fossils** were first found in the 1780s. Many more have been found since!

Today's tree sloths are related to giant ground sloths. Like ground sloths, tree sloths have long fur and claws. But they are smaller. They live in trees.

GIANT GROUND SLOTH

larger size

long fur

lived on the ground and in burrows

long claws

Giant ground sloths are gone.
But other sloths live on!

TREE SLOTH

long fur

long claws

live in trees

smaller size

GET TO KNOW THE GIANT GROUND SLOTH

long fur

DIET

leaves

grass

fruit

meat

strong back legs

short tail

WEIGHT

more than 8,000 pounds
(3,629 kilograms)

20

WHEN DID THEY LIVE?

around 35 million years ago
Giant ground sloths first appear

160,000 to 90,000 years ago
Early modern humans first appear

around 10,000 years ago
Giant ground sloths begin to go extinct

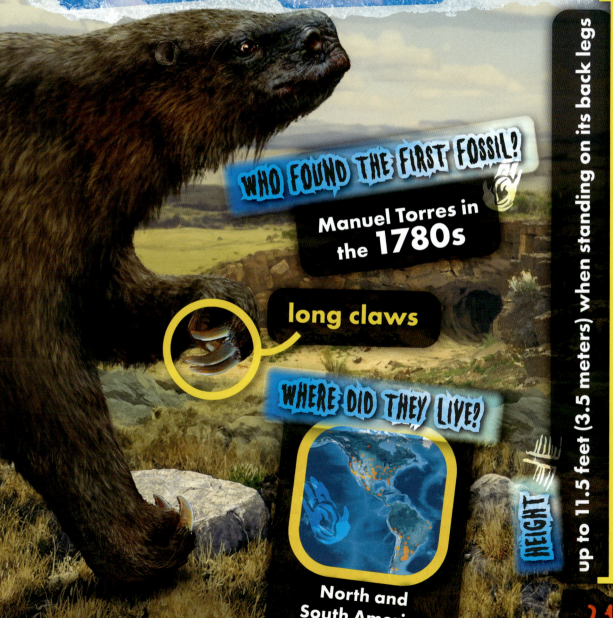

WHO FOUND THE FIRST FOSSIL?

Manuel Torres in the 1780s

long claws

WHERE DID THEY LIVE?

North and South America

HEIGHT

up to 11.5 feet (3.5 meters) when standing on its back legs

21

GLOSSARY

balance—to move or stay in the same place without losing control or falling

burrows—holes or tunnels in the ground that some animals dig for homes

climate—the usual weather conditions in a certain place

Eocene epoch—a geological time period that began around 56 million years ago and ended around 33.9 million years ago

extinct—no longer living

fossils—the remains of living things that lived long ago

herbivores—animals that only eat plants

mammals—warm-blooded animals that have backbones and feed their young milk

omnivores—animals that eat both plants and animals

predators—animals that hunt other animals for food

species—types of an animal

TO LEARN MORE

AT THE LIBRARY

Gleisner, Jenna Lee. *If I Gardened With a Giant Ground Sloth.* Minneapolis, Minn.: Jump!, 2023.

Kenney, Karen Latchana. *Sloths.* Minneapolis, Minn.: Bellwether Media, 2021.

King, SJ. *The Secret Explorers and the Ice Age Adventure.* New York, N.Y.: DK Publishing, 2022.

ON THE WEB

FACTSURFER

Factsurfer.com gives you a safe, fun way to find more information.

1. Go to www.factsurfer.com.

2. Enter "giant ground sloths" into the search box and click 🔍 .

3. Select your book cover to see a list of related content.

INDEX